THE ROSE PRINCESS
AND OTHER PLAYS

Borgo Press Books by FRANK J. MORLOCK

Castor and Pollux and Other Opera Libretti (Editor)
The Chevalier d'Éon and Other Short Farces (Editor)
Chuzzlewit
Congreve's Comedy of Manners
Crime and Punishment
Cyrano and Molière: Five Plays by or About Molière (Editor)
Doctor Scratch and Other Plays (Editor)
Falstaff (with Shakespeare, John Dennis, & William Kendrick)
Fathers and Sons
Herculaneum & Sardanapalus: Two Opera Libretti (Editor)
The Idiot
Isle of Slaves and Other Plays (Editor)
Jurgen
Justine
The Key to the Great Gate and Other Plays
The Londoners & The Green Carnation: Two Plays
Lord Jim
Mademoiselle Fifi and Other Plays (Editor)
The Madwoman of Beresina & Other Napoleonic Plays (Editor)
Mimi Pinson and Other Plays (Editor)
Notes from the Underground
Oblomov
Old Creole Days
Outrageous Women: Lady Macbeth and Other Plays (Editor)
Parades and Proverbs: Eight Plays (Editor)
Peter and Alexis
The Princess Casamassima
A Raw Youth
The Rose Princess and Other Plays
Salammbô & Dido: Two Operas (Editor)
The Stendhal Hamlet Scenarios and Other Shakespearean Shorts from the French (Editor)
Two Voltairean Plays: The Triumvirate; Comedy at Ferney
Whitewashing Julia and Other Plays
The Widow's Husband; and, Porthos in Search of an Outfit: Two Dumasian Comedies (Editor)
A Yiddish Hamlet and Other Plays
Zeneida & The Follies of Love & The Cat Who Changed into a Woman: Two Plays (Editor)

THE ROSE PRINCESS AND OTHER PLAYS

FRANK J. MORLOCK

THE BORGO PRESS
MMXIII

THE ROSE PRINCESS AND OTHER PLAYS

Copyright © 1985, 1999, 2013 by Frank J. Morlock

FIRST EDITION

Published by Wildside Press LLC

www.wildsidebooks.com

DEDICATION

To the Memory of My Late Uncle,
Paris Pierson

CONTENTS

THE ROSE PRINCESS 9
CAST OF CHARACTERS. 10
THE PLAY 11
BETTER LUCK NEXT TIME. 67
CAST OF CHARACTERS. 68
THE PLAY 69
CHRISTMAS AT THOMPSON HALL. 80
CAST OF CHARACTERS. 81
THE PLAY 82
FROGGY 95
CAST OF CHARACTERS. 96
THE PLAY 97
THE GOLDEN GOBLIN. 129
CAST OF CHARACTERS. 130
THE PLAY 131
REHEARSING DON QUIXOTE 165
CAST OF CHARACTERS. 166

THE PLAY	167
ROBERT THE DEVIL	177
CAST OF CHARACTERS	178
THE PLAY	180
ABOUT THE AUTHOR	221

THE ROSE PRINCESS
A PLAY BASED ON A FAIRY TALE

CAST OF CHARACTERS

THE KING

QUEEN FLORA

THE FAIRY TITANIA

PRINCESS ROSEBUD

ARDRAM

ARDRAM'S MOTHER

DOCTOR MAX

SCENE I

A garden in the palace.

QUEEN:

Woe is me. I am childless. If only I had a child.

KING:

A boy would be nice.

QUEEN:

A girl would be better!

KING:

We need an heir to the throne.

QUEEN:

You men are all alike.

KING:

Any child would be nice.

QUEEN:

Well, do something!

KING:

I suppose we could keep trying.

QUEEN:

Of, course that's just what you want. Try and try again. Men! Don't you know some doctor who could bring this about?

KING:

We've tried all the doctors.

QUEEN:

Well then, a magician?

KING:

We've tried all the magicians.

QUEEN:

Maybe not the good ones.

KING:

Merlin, Faustus, the lot.

QUEEN:

How about a fairy?

KING:

Sorry. Don't know any! My great-grandfather was the last mortal ever to see a fairy. No one has ever seen one since.

QUEEN:

Humph! They probably don't exist anyway.

KING:

Well, they say this palace was built by fairy hands.

QUEEN:

You believe anything. Absolutely anything. If they existed, wouldn't they want to help me have a baby?

KING:

Why? I don't really see the connection.

QUEEN:

Oh, you are so stupid.

KING:

Possibly because I am King.

QUEEN:

Shut up. Look, you are King, right?

KING:

Absolutely. I'm an absolute monarch.

QUEEN:

And I am Queen, right?

KING:

Roger that.

QUEEN:

And we have no child.

KING:

Right. (aside) Actually, I have a few dozen bastards here and there, but they don't count, and I must remember not to mention them to the Queen.

QUEEN:

Well, if there were fairies, the fairies would naturally want to help the King and the Queen to be happy. Everybody knows that.

KING:

Um.

QUEEN:

What's the good of having fairies if they are no use to you when you need them? Answer me that!

KING:

Um.

QUEEN:

So there aren't any! So there!

KING:

Well, if there are any, I could surely use some help. The people are restive. There may be a revolution.

QUEEN:

Revolution! Pooh!

KING:

Well, the people don't have any bread to eat.

QUEEN:

Let them eat cake!

KING:

That's a good idea.

QUEEN:

I have many good ideas, but you never pay any attention to them.

KING:

Well, that one is a real crackerjack. I'm going to tell the Chancellor to suggest that the next time there's a bread riot.

QUEEN:

Things are so simple really.

KING:

I just don't want to have a revolution. I like being King.

QUEEN:

And I like being Queen. What's a revolution, anyway?

KING:

That's when the people depose the King and Queen.

QUEEN:

I'd like to see them try that! Just you wait.

KING:

Actually, my grandfather became King during a revolution.

QUEEN:

How dreadful.

KING:

Actually, it turned out well for me and my father, too.

QUEEN:

I suppose, from that narrow point of view. But I am a legitimist. Whatever that is.

KING:

Now I think on it, it was the fairies helped him to the

throne.

QUEEN:

Humbug!

KING:

They say some of the descendants of the old King are still living in the city.

QUEEN:

A likely story.

KING:

Protected by the fairies.

QUEEN:

And the secret police?

KING:

The secret police have never been able to find them—but they are sure those descendants are there.

QUEEN:

I don't believe a word of it.

KING:

If it weren't for the fairies, my secret police would have exterminated them by now. I've got a very nasty secret police.

QUEEN:

But for the fairies? Fairies indeed! Tell the head of the secret police you are going to hang him if he doesn't find the descendants of the old King. You see how quick they find someone to exterminate.

KING:

That's a thought. But if there really are fairies—

QUEEN:

Fairies do not exist!

KING:

There's no reasoning with you. I'm going to an important cabinet meeting.

QUEEN:

They don't exist and that's my last word on the subject! Now what's the cabinet meeting about?

KING:

Ah, now there you have me. I've forgotten. Oh, wait, I remember. It's about how to raise taxes to build a 400-room extension to the palace and new means of helping the poor.

QUEEN:

Boring! Make it 500 rooms. And a new palace in the country.

KING:

All right. Can I have a kiss before I go?

QUEEN:

Don't touch me! (she pulls away and folds her arms over her breast)

KING:

What did I do?

QUEEN:

It's what you didn't do.

KING:

What didn't I do?

QUEEN:

You didn't make me have a baby and you can't touch me until you do.

KING:

But, how can I—

QUEEN:

You'll be late for your meeting. (imperiously) Go!

KING:

Oh, very well.

QUEEN:

And remember, 500 rooms. No make it six.

KING:

All right. That will only require tripling the taxes. Back in a flash. (exit King)

QUEEN:

Don't rush! (irritated, the Queen goes around kicking over chairs, knocking over flower posta, anything she can destroy in her anger; exhausted, she sits down, grabs some flowers, and begins pulling them apart)

There are no fairies! You hear? There are no fairies! (she tosses the flowers)

VOICE:

(laughing) Yes, there are.

QUEEN:

Who said that?

VOICE:

Ha, ha, ha —

QUEEN:

You'd better watch it. I am capable of having your head severed from your body in the mood I'm in. So be careful. I can be a real bitch when I'm mad.

VOICE:

I believe you.

QUEEN:

(starts looking for the owner of the voice) You're going to get it.

VOICE:

So, you don't believe in fairies?

QUEEN:

No. Where are you?

VOICE:

Over here.

QUEEN:

(peering into a rosebush) My goodness. You are a fairy. You're so small.

ROSEBUD:

(suddenly appearing) I can be any size I please.

QUEEN:

Goodness. A real fairy. My husband will never believe this.

QUEEN:

My name's Rosina. (curtsies) Howdja do?

QUEEN

(bowing graciously in return) Very pleased to meet

you, Miss Rosina. Should I call you Miss? What's your title, anyway? Will you give me a baby?

ROSINA:

Normally, we don't get mixed up in family planning.

QUEEN:

Oh, but I am Queen.

ROSINA:

But being Queen doesn't automatically mean you will have a baby.

QUEEN:

But I'm a good Queen.

ROSINA:

(astounded) You think so?

QUEEN:

I know so. I have the most wonderful balls —

ROSINA:

The most expensive, the most lavish ever seen.

QUEEN:

You see! And all my people love me.

ROSINA:

Do they? I have a different impression.

QUEEN:

Oh, you can't be paying attention. Every report from the secret police emphasizes how attached the people are to me. They don't care much for my husband though. He lacks charm and charisma.

ROSINA:

Hmmmm! Actually, considering the political conditions in the realm, I think it would be a very good idea if there was an heir to the throne.

QUEEN:

Then you'll grant my wish?

ROSINA:

Yes.

QUEEN:

So nice of you. I knew right away I could trust you.

ROSINA:

You see, there may be a revolution.

QUEEN:

A revolution. Unthinkable! I won't allow it. I'm the only Queen these stupid people have got.

ROSINA:

That's why it would be nice to have an alternative. (plucking a rosebud.) Now, put this rosebud in your bed tonight, and in the morning you will have a beautiful little baby Princess.

QUEEN:

Neat! I'll call her Rosebud.

ROSINA:

Very original of you. But every night at sundown, the Princess will change back into a flower.

QUEEN:

Now, wait a minute.

ROSINA:

Not to worry. At sunrise she will be human again.

QUEEN:

A curious child. Is this going to go on forever?

ROSINA:

Only until she marries the great-grandson of the old King.

QUEEN:

You mean the one my husband's grandfather deposed?

ROSINA:

Exactly.

QUEEN:

I'll have them married tomorrow.

ROSINA:

Can't do that! He hasn't actually been born yet. Besides, he won't know he's of royal blood until Rosebud tells him.

QUEEN:

And after they get married, she'll be a Princess day and night?

ROSINA:

Yes.

QUEEN:

I don't see how she's ever going to find him. I shall certainly not allow my child to scour the world looking for him.

ROSINA:

Fate is stronger than you are. You will see what you will see.

(Rosina disappears.)

QUEEN:

Now where'd she go? What a strange and complicated story? Well, at least I'll have the baby I always wanted.

(Enter the King.)

KING:

Well, that's all over. We've got our new palace. Our loyal subjects voted to triple their tax burden. The Royal Architect will be over to see you this afternoon.

QUEEN:

Oh, I can't be bothered with that.

KING:

Huh? I thought —

QUEEN:

It doesn't interest me anymore.

KING:

Damn! But we just doubled the national debt!

QUEEN:

Never mind. I'm going to have a baby.

KING:

You mean you're pregnant? (gestures suggesting a fat tummy)

QUEEN:

No, stupid! (showing the rosebud) In the morning this rosebud will turn into a baby.

KING:

Stop kidding.

QUEEN:

I'm not kidding. A fairy gave it to me.

KING:

A fairy, eh? Did you fall asleep out here?

QUEEN:

Are you suggesting I've been dreaming?

KING:

Um, yes.

QUEEN:

Well I've been wide awake. I met a fairy.

KING:

There are no fairies.

QUEEN:

There are so.

KING:

You've been in the sun too long.

QUEEN:

There are fairies.

KING:

Maybe you ought to go lie down.

QUEEN:

That's a good idea. Come with me.

KING:

Huh?

QUEEN:

We can—you know.

KING:

I thought you weren't going to let me touch you until—?

QUEEN:

But that's all arranged. I don't have it on my mind any more, so—

KING:

Then I can—?

QUEEN:

Yes, you can—in fact, I insist.

KING:

Well I'll be damned. How did this come about?

QUEEN:

(snuggling up to him) The fairies, I told you.

KING:

But there are no fairies.

QUEEN:

You just like to contradict me. If I weren't in such a good mood, I'd never let you touch me again ever. Now, repeat after me. There are fairies.

KING:

There are fairies.

(The King and Queen kiss.)

BLACKOUT

SCENE II

The Palace garden, seventeen years later.

The fairy Rosina leads in Princess Rosebud. The palace hasn't changed much, except that there are revolutionary flags hanging, a few heads on pikes, and a large guillotine in the background.

ROSINA:

Don't weep, Princess. Things will all come out right.

ROSEBUD:

But my dear parents. The people want to cut off their heads.

ROSINA:

They've escaped with the help of some friends of mine.

ROSEBUD:

Oh, what a relief.

ROSINA:

But they must learn to suffer. When they have learned their lesson, they will come back again.

ROSEBUD:

But what will become of me?

ROSINA:

Don't worry: you'll be safe enough. In the end the people who are now screaming for your head will cheer you on your wedding day.

ROSEBUD:

That's interesting. I wonder who I'll marry.

ROSINA:

Oh, you'll find out. Meanwhile, I must save you from the people, or they will certainly kill you.

(Peasants rush in with scythes, axes, etc. Rosina and Rosebud vanish in a puff of smoke.)

BLACKOUT

SCENE III

Ardram's room. The dimly lit room of a poor student. Books everywhere. A banner saying, "Long live the revolution". Another: "Down with tyranny!" Ardram is writing at his desk. There is a noise. Ardram turns and sees Rosebud standing bewildered by his bed. Ardram is stunned.

ARDRAM:

Who are you?

ROSEBUD:

I'm Princess Rosebud.

ARDRAM:

How did you get in here?

ROSEBUD:

I have no idea. Will you let me stay?

ARDRAM:

(looking at her) Yes.

ROSEBUD:

I'm afraid of the mob that broke into the palace.

ARDRAM:

I…I won't let them harm you.

ROSEBUD:

How can you protect me?

ARDRAM:

I'm their leader!

ROSEBUD:

You! (terrified, she wants to flee, but she doesn't know where the door is)

ARDRAM:

(going to her) Don't be afraid. We revolutionaries don't want to harm anyone. We just want justice.

ROSEBUD:

But they're killing everybody.

ARDRAM:

The people are a little too enthusiastic at the moment, but they'll calm down.

ROSEBUD:

What will happen?

ARDRAM:

The Constituent Assembly will establish a constitutional monarchy.

ROSEBUD:

A constitutional monarchy! What's that?

ARDRAM:

It's a kind of monarchy that isn't really a monarchy. So far, it's only existed in England.

ROSEBUD:

But who will be King? Will you put my father back on the throne?

ARDRAM:

Impossible. His tyrannies are too fresh in the minds of the people. The people will have to offer the crown to someone else.

ROSEBUD:

Who?

ARDRAM:

Don't know yet. We have to find someone.

ROSEBUD:

Well, you're their leader. Perhaps they'll offer the throne to you?

ARDRAM:

I don't think so. I'm not sure I approve of monarchy anyway. We need someone who will make sure the people have enough bread to eat.

ROSEBUD:

My father says that's impossible.

ARDRAM:

Your father, dear Princess, is an ass.

ROSEBUD:

Don't you talk like that about my father!

ARDRAM:

I don't have time to argue with you. I have to go to a Revolutionary meeting.

ROSEBUD:

But—

ARDRAM:

I really have to go. Things might really get out of hand if I don't. There are some crazies who want to establish a democracy.

ROSEBUD:

Oh, dear. That must be prevented at all costs.

ARDRAM:

And then there's the matter of dealing with the aristocrats.

ROSEBUD:

Please look out for my parents.

ARDRAM:

The best thing would be if no one found them right now. (starts to leave)

ROSEBUD:

Young man!

ARDRAM:

Yes?

ROSEBUD:

What's your name?

ARDRAM:

Ardram.

ROSEBUD:

That's a nice name.

ARDRAM:

What's yours?

ROSEBUD:

Rosebud.

ARDRAM:

That's a strange name for a Princess.

ROSEBUD:

My mother calls me Rosie and my father calls me Buddy.

ARDRAM:

I like Buddy. It's got a revolutionary sound to it. Look, whatever you do, don't leave. I cannot protect you if you leave.

ROSEBUD:

I'll be here, Ardram.

ARDRAM:

See you later, Buddy.

(He goes out. Rosebud sits in his chair and starts reading a revolutionary pamphlet with surprise and attention.)

BLACKOUT

SCENE IV

When the lights come back up, it is late at night. Ardram is writing at his desk furiously. No sign of Rosebud. The door opens and Ardram's mother enters.

MOTHER:

How's my son, the Revolutionary?

ARDRAM:

I'm good, mother.

MOTHER:

And the Revolution?

ARDRAM:

Not so good. Aside from cutting off the heads of aristocrats, no one is able to agree on anything.

MOTHER:

The people need a leader.

ARDRAM:

There's going to be a civil war.

MOTHER:

No way.

ARDRAM:

But—

MOTHER:

A civil war is out of the question. We must find someone of royal blood to be a constitutional monarch.

ARDRAM:

(laughing) How about the one who's protected by the fairies?

MOTHER:

The ideal person.

ARDRAM:

If only we could find him.

MOTHER:

(looking around and finding a rose in Ardram's bed)

Where did this come from?

ARDRAM:

Beats me. (thinking) Maybe Buddy put it there.

MOTHER:

Buddy! Who is Buddy?

ARDRAM:

She's a young girl who showed up here this morning.

MOTHER:

She showed up?

ARDRAM:

That's the only way to describe it. I was sitting here working and there she was.

MOTHER:

Buddy is an unusual name for a girl.

ARDRAM:

Her real name is Rosie or something, but her friends call her Buddy.

MOTHER:

(more and more uneasy) And you are her "friend"?

ARDRAM:

I guess so.

MOTHER:

Now, I've always told you you mustn't get involved with some peasant girl.

ARDRAM:

I'm not involved with her and she's not a peasant.

MOTHER:

It leads to "complications." You mustn't—

ARDRAM:

Wait a minute. Where is Buddy? I told her not to go out. It's dangerous and I may not be able to protect her.

MOTHER:

You protect her! My God, this is serious.

ARDRAM:

Buddy! Buddy, where are you?

(Buddy, of course, having turned into a rose, does not answer. Ardram suddenly becomes frantic. He looks all over the room and an adjoining room. He is staring wildly.)

ARDRAM:

I've got to find her! Stay here, mother. (he rushes out screaming) Buddy! Buddy! Where are you?

MOTHER:

Oh, dear, I'm afraid this may be serious. It's so unwise to form a misalliance.

BLACKOUT

SCENE V

When the lights go up, it is early morning in Ardram's room. Ardram's mother is sleeping on a couch. Rosebud sits up in the bed. She looks around and sees Ardram's mother sleeping on the couch.

ROSEBUD:

Excuse me for waking you up. (she nudges Ardram's mother, who sits up) But, who are you?

MOTHER:

Are you "Buddy"?

ROSEBUD:

My father calls me that.

MOTHER:

(looking at her critically) Well, you are not bad-looking for some peasant slut. In fact, you have the bearing of a Princess.

ROSEBUD:

I— (about to say "I am a Princess," she thinks better of it and bites her tongue)

MOTHER:

Well, how much do you want to clear out?

ROSEBUD:

What do you mean?

MOTHER:

How much do you want to beat it and find some other man?

ROSEBUD:

But—

ARDRAM:

I suppose you may have some attachment for him. I must seem a little brutal. I am sure you mean well enough, but my son must not become involved with a wench like you.

ROSEBUD:

A wench like me! I AM PRINCESS ROSEBUD!

MOTHER:

You're Princess Rosebud?

ROSEBUD:

Yes.

MOTHER:

Well then, that's another matter. Why did you leave? Why did you run away?

ROSEBUD:

I didn't run away.

MOTHER:

He's been searching for you everywhere. He hasn't come home yet. You wicked girl, running around the streets all night.

ROSEBUD:

I was not.

MOTHER:

Then where did you go?

ROSEBUD:

I can't explain very well. If I told you, you wouldn't believe me.

MOTHER:

I expect so. Look here: do you love my son?

ROSEBUD:

I don't know. I just met him.

MOTHER:

Well, it doesn't matter whether you love him or not. Will you marry him?

ROSEBUD:

But he's a commoner. I suppose that's an advantage these days. Yes, I'll do it.

MOTHER:

That's a good girl. I'm beginning to like you already.

ROSEBUD:

But I don't think he likes me very much. After all, he's a Red Republican, a fanatic revolutionary, and all that. What would he want with a Princess? Besides, I'm betrothed to the lost Prince of the Old Dynasty. That is, if he's ever found.

MOTHER:

No problem. Ardram is the great-grandson of King Ardram the Stupid, my ancestor. So if you marry him, he will regain the throne.

ROSEBUD:

And my father and mother?

MOTHER:

A comfortable exile is the best I can do for them. The people wouldn't tolerate them again.

BLACKOUT

SCENE VI

Doctor Max's house.

QUEEN:

Doctor Max, Doctor Max. What is going on in the city?

DOCTOR MAX:

As I came through the streets, I noticed that there was a growing sentiment to reestablish the monarchy.

KING:

It's about time.

QUEEN:

I told you this revolution thing would never last.

KING:

Far too long for my liking already. Here we are, hiding in Doctor Max's humble abode.

QUEEN:

With no servants.

KING:

And no hunting. It's very dreadful.

QUEEN:

At last we will be able to return to our palace.

KING:

What an example I am going to make of all those traitors.

DOCTOR MAX:

I said there is sentiment to reestablish the monarchy, Sire. I didn't say there was any sentiment to put you back on the throne.

KING:

Nonsense. I'm the only King they've got.

QUEEN:

The people grow more ridiculous every day. Where else will they get a King?

MAX:

They want to put your daughter on the throne!

QUEEN:

Without our being dead? How dare they.

MAX:

Listen.

SHOUTS:

Long live Queen Rosebud the first. Where is the brat? We didn't kill her, did we?

QUEEN:

Ah, my poor daughter, Indeed, where is she? I haven't seen her since the day that mob invaded the palace.

MAX:

She'll be easy to recognize.

KING:

I'm not so sure of that. Princess Rosebud is protected by fairies.

DOCTOR MAX:

Protected by fairies? I never saw one.

QUEEN:

But I did.

DOCTOR MAX:

Excuse me, Highness, dyspepsia.

QUEEN:

(aside to King) I'd like to tell this little know-it-all Doctor off. In fact, I'd like to have his head chopped off, the insolent little beast. To contradict me. Me, his Queen. But I don't dare. He might turn us over to the mob.

KING:

I feel the same way, but in this case discretion is advisable.

ARDRAM'S VOICE:

Good People. Elect Princess Rosebud as Queen.

KING:

The seditious traitor.

QUEEN:

Cut off his head!

DOCTOR MAX:

That's Ardram, the student, who is the leader of the Constituent Assembly.

QUEEN:

I always told you that founding the University was a mistake. But you wouldn't listen. Education breeds sedition, revolution, anarchy, I don't know what.

(Rosebud suddenly appears.)

ROSEBUD:

Mama! Papa!

(Rosebud runs to embrace them.)

QUEEN:

How did you get here? You weren't here a minute ago.

ROSEBUD:

I don't know. I've had so many adventures. I was so afraid the mob had killed you!

KING:

They most certainly would have, had it not been for the kindness of Doctor Max, who has hidden us. If I ever become King again, I'll show him all my gratitude.

QUEEN:

And mine! But we were so worried about you.

KING:

The people are offering to put you on the throne in place of us.

QUEEN:

They are trying to use you.

KING:

Especially this Ardram, this rabble rouser, this butcher.

ROSEBUD:

I know all about that. My job is to marry the Lost Prince, and break the spell. Then I'll be a real Princess, not just a daytime Princess.

QUEEN:

When you marry him, it will break the spell. But how

to find him?

ROSEBUD:

Piece of cake, I've already found him. Ardram is the lost prince.

KING:

Ardram! Don't be ridiculous. He's just a rabble-rousing demagogue.

QUEEN:

An impossible alliance. You must be mistaken.

ROSEBUD:

There's no mistake. His mother, who is a direct descendant of King Ardram the Stupid, told me so.

QUEEN:

And what proof does she have?

ROSEBUD:

She gave me the lost crown of King Ardram. See, here. (gives her father a crown)

KING:

(examining it carefully) Well this looks like the real thing. It's very carefully described in the archives and there are pictures of it in several mosaics. Better marry this dude right away and break this enchantment.

ROSEBUD:

Yes, but where is he?

DOCTOR MAX:

He's coming down the street at the head of the mob.

ROSEBUD:

Ardram, Ardram, I am here.

VOICES:

Long live Queen Rosebud.

ROSEBUD:

(opening the door) And King Ardram. If you make me Queen, you must make him King. And we will both rule very wisely.

KING:

What about us?

QUEEN:

She never thinks of us.

KING:

Just like kids nowadays.

ROSINA:

(appearing) Well, are you sorry you lost your throne?

KING:

Extremely.

QUEEN:

Terribly.

ROSINA:

If you are restored, will you rule wisely?

KING AND QUEEN:

Just as wisely as we did before.

ROSINA:

And will you take care of your subjects?

KING AND QUEEN:

Just as we did in the past.

ROSINA:

Then you are incorrigible!

QUEEN:

Absolutely. (to King) What's incorruptible mean?

ROSINA:

You are not fit to rule.

KING:

If I wasn't fit to rule, why did God make me a King?

ROSINA:

You'll never learn.

QUEEN:

The King is right.

KING:

You see, she can't answer that one.

ROSINA:

I had hoped to reform you.

KING:

Reform me? That's pretty presumptuous.

QUEEN:

Nonsense!

KING:

Is that rabble-rouser really a Prince?

ROSINA:

Yes, he is.

KING:

Well, I suppose he'll do for a son-in-law then. But we don't really want a Red in the family. We've got enough skeletons in the family closet.

QUEEN:

Yes. Your father for example.

KING:

Never mind my father.

QUEEN:

He was mad.

KING:

Forget about that.

ROSINA:

I am the Queen of the Fairies and I have come to put things right. (she waves her wand and the crowd which was clamoring falls obediently silent) Now, Prince Ardram—

ARDRAM:

Why do you call me Prince Ardram? I am citizen Ardram.

ROSINA:

Princess Rosebud will explain.

ROSEBUD:

You are the great-grandson of King Ardram the Stupid.

ARDRAM:

(to his Mother, who has just entered) Mother, is this true?

MOTHER:

Perfectly true, my child. But I couldn't tell you until Queen Rosina gave me permission.

ROSINA:

And I waited until now so that all these disorders could be calmed by your marriage to Princess Rosebud.

ROSEBUD AND ARDRAM:

You want us to get married?

ROSINA:

Your marriage will reunite the old monarchy with the new and calm the revolutionary fervors of the masses forever by creating a constitutional monarchy.

ARDRAM AND ROSEBUD:

When must we marry?

ROSINA:

Now.

(A wedding march suddenly breaks out.)

KING AND QUEEN:

That's all very well, but what is to become of us?

QUEEN:

Yes. What is to become of us?

ROSINA:

You only care about yourselves and living a life of pleasure. You must go to France where the people are as fond of pleasure as you are. There you will be happy.

KING:

That's ridiculous.

QUEEN:

I agree, but Paris is nice.

KING:

(aside) The mamzelles are pretty.

VOICES:

Long live King Ardram and Queen Rosebud!

(Ardram and Rosebud go out to the acclamation of the crowd.)

DOCTOR MAX:

(To Rosina) A Question. What makes you think Rosebud and Ardram will make better monarchs than the present King and Queen?

ROSINA:

Why they are young, idealistic, and they mean well.

DOCTOR MAX:

I'm old enough to remember when the King and the Queen, for that matter, were young, idealistic, and meant well. And you see what happened.

ROSINA:

(thinking about it) I see your point. But there's a difference. This is a fairy tale.

DOCTOR MAX:

Ah! Say no more!

CURTAIN

BETTER LUCK NEXT TIME
Adapted from a Story by Arlo Bates

CAST OF CHARACTERS

Members of the Soldiers' Aid Society:

Mrs. Cumings

Mrs. Drew

Mrs. Stern

Mattie Seaton, a young flirt

Non-speaking roles:

Archie

Nancy

Mary

Delia Burrage

THE PLAY

A graveyard with a large gravestone, sometime during the American Civil War. Soldiers and people cross the stage in mourning. It is a Sunday afternoon.

Three middle-aged women members of the Soldiers' Aid Society are looking at the newly erected gravestone of Archie Lovell.

MRS. CUMINGS

Well, Old Lady Andrews did right nice by Archie. It's the fanciest tombstone in Cedarville.

MRS. STERN

She was always an old fool about her nephew anyway.

MRS. DREW

It's an awful shame his body was never found. Poor Archie's probably in some ditch. It makes me shiver.

MRS. CUMINGS

I wonder why she went to Boston so sudden.

MRS. STERN

It's none of your business, Nellie Cumings, nor mine neither. I expect she had some business.

MRS. DREW

At least she's spared the spectacle of three girls puttin' on mournin' for Archie.

MRS. STERN

For my part, I don't believe any one of the three was ever really engaged to Archie Lovell. He went round with all of them, of course, but that wasn't anything—with him!

MRS. DREW

I expect it's very easy for a girl to put on mourning when a man's dead and she says she's been engaged to him!

MRS. STERN

If any one of 'em had been engaged to Archie Lovell while he was alive, she'd have bragged enough about it at the time.

MRS. CUMINGS

A soldier can never tell these days who'll take it into her head to claim she was betrothed to him.

MRS. DREW

The way things are going, the men are getting killed off so fast that the only satisfaction a girl can get anyway is to go into mourning for some of 'em, and I don't blame 'em if they do it!

MRS. STERN

Let's hope they don't present the parish with a passel of brats.

MRS. DREW

Sarah Stern! What a thing to say.

MRS. STERN

Fiddlesticks. It won't be the first brat we've had since this war started.

MRS. DREW

If it was one of the three, it was Delia Burrage. He used to go around with her all the time.

MRS. CUMINGS

No more'n he did with Mattie Seaton. He used to see Mattie home from singing school that winter before he enlisted!

MRS. DREW

Well, anyway, when Delia presented the flag to the militia before they marched off, he was with her all evening.

MRS. CUMINGS

He used to go with Mattie a lot.

MRS. STERN

He sent Mary Foster that wooden chair he carved.

MRS. CUMINGS

Well, that was on a bet. That don't count. She told me so herself.

MRS. STERN

I don't know how many girls Archie was engaged to—I dare say he didn't know himself—and for all I know, he may have been engaged to all three of these girls that are flying the black flag for him. But I can tell you the girl he really wanted to marry—and she isn't in black either.

MRS. CUMINGS

Who is it?

MRS. DREW

I don't know who there is that's any more likely to have been engaged to him than Mattie.

MRS. STERN

He'd no more have married her than he would me.

MRS. DREW

Who is it then?

MRS. STERN

Nancy Turner.

MRS. CUMINGS

She's a sly one—

MRS. DREW

Look, here comes Delia.

(The three gossips draw back. Delia Burrage, decked out in her best crape, goes up to the tombstone and arranges some flowers. Everyone stares.)

MRS. CUMINGS

Here comes Mary Foster.

(Mary, also carrying flowers sails up, and, not to be outdone, falls on her knees. Delia, not to be outshone, does so also. But Mary has gained the upper hand.)

MRS. STERN

Now we'll have a show, here comes Mattie!

Mrs. CUMINGS

Trust Mattie Seaton for not letting anybody get ahead of her.

(Mattie approaches, flinging back her long veil to reveal her pretty face. Then in a deliberately loud voice)

MATTIE

Oh, thank you so much for bringing flowers. Archie was so fond of them!

(Mattie moves behind the tombstone and places a wreath she is carrying over it. This leaves her standing with her two rivals kneeling.)

MRS. DREW

Is she boss of that grave or not, I ask you?

MRS. CUMINGS

If that ain't the beatinest.

MRS. STERN

I wish Archie Lovell could see that. He'd be more than willing to get killed for a sight of his three widders and that Seaton girl comin' in so over the others.

MRS. DREW

He'd think he was a Mormon or a Turk.

MRS. CUMINGS

He'd see the fun of it. Poor Archie, he did love a joke.

MATTIE (in a broken voice)

Thank you so much for your sympathy.

(Mattie, after kissing the top of the tombstone, exits dramatically in tears. Delia and Mary exchange a furious glance, but unable to think of a retort, get to their feet almost as one and beat a retreat in a different direction. The old gossips cannot restrain themselves and begin to laugh.)

MRS. DREW

God forgive me, I can't help laughin'.

MRS. CUMINGS

Well, where's Nancy Turner?

MRS. DREW

She didn't feel well enough to come this afternoon.

MRS. STERN

She's with Old Lady Andrews.

MRS. DREW

Old Lady Andrews got home?

MRS. STERN

Yes, this noon.

MRS. CUMINGS

But, you said she'd gone to Boston.

MRS. STERN

Nobody knew but me.

MRS. DREW (soberly)

Did she bring home Archie's body?

MRS. STERN

Yes, she did. She had a dreadful time finding out anything, but she has friends in Washington.

MRS. DREW

Where was Archie buried?

MRS. STERN

He wasn't buried anywhere.

MRS. DREW

Why not?

MRS. STERN

'Cause he ain't dead.

MRS. CUMINGS

Not dead!

MRS. STERN

No, only taken prisoner. He was wounded and he's been in Andersonville.

MRS. DREW

How is he now?

MRS. STERN

Oh, he's all right now. And here he comes, to see his gravestone.

(A Union Lieutenant and a girl in crinoline come in, arm in arm.)

MRS. CUMINGS

Why, it's Nancy Turner with him.

MRS. STERN

No, it's Nancy Lovell. They were married in Boston.

(A crowd has gathered. Miss Burrage and Miss Foster try to hide, but Mattie Seaton daringly comes forward.)

MATTIE

Why, Archie dear, we thought we had lost you forever. We all supposed you were dead, and here you are, only married. Let me congratulate you, though after being engaged to so many girls, it must seem queer to be married to only one. Nancy, to think you got him after all, just because you went ahead and caught him! I congratulate you with all my heart, only look out for him. He'll make love to any woman he sees. (she kisses the speechless Nancy) Come Delia, come Mary! There's nothing for us to do but to go home and take off our black. We may have better luck next time!

(Mattie sails out with Delia and Mary in tow.)

MRS. DREW

Did you ever!

Mrs. CUMINGS

This is a scandal.

MRS. STERN

Now, that girl has grit!

CURTAIN

CHRISTMAS AT THOMPSON HALL

Adapted from a Story
by Anthony Trollope

CAST OF CHARACTERS

Mrs. Brown

Mr. Brown

Mr. Jones

Bellboy

SCENE I

An English hotel room in the middle of the nineteenth century.

MR. BROWN:

If I can't get something to relieve me, I know I shall never make my way on.

MRS. BROWN:

But my dear, what can I do? What can I do, my dearie? You know I would do anything if I could. Get into bed, my pet, and be warm, and then tomorrow morning you will be all right.

MR. BROWN:

I'll tell you what you can do. Go down to the desk and get me a jar of (whispers bashfully). But I am afraid it will be very disagreeable for you to go down all alone at this time of night.

MRS. BROWN:

Of course, I'll go. I don't mind going in the least. I won't be two minutes, my darling.

BLACKOUT

SCENE II

The Hotel Room sometime later that night.

MRS. BROWN

(opening the door hesitantly and seeing her husband still up, comes in) Oh, my dear, why are you not in bed? Why did you get up? I left you warm and comfortable.

MR. BROWN:

Where have you been all night?

MRS. BROWN:

I've been looking for the (whispers with embarrassment).

MR. BROWN:

Have you been looking all night and haven't found it? Where have you been?

MRS. BROWN:

I got badly lost in the corridors.

MR. BROWN:

Surely there must have been someone about the hotel? You can't possibly have been lost all these hours?

MRS. BROWN:

Only about one hour, my dear. I got the porter to help me.

MR. BROWN:

Why didn't you tell him what you wanted?

MRS. BROWN:

(aghast) My dear?

MR. BROWN:

Why not? Nothing to be ashamed of.

MRS. BROWN:

At one o'clock in the morning? I couldn't do it. To tell the truth, he wasn't very civil. I thought he was a little tipsy. Now, my dear, go to bed.

MR. BROWN:

Why didn't you get the (whispers)?

MRS. BROWN:

There wasn't any. I searched everywhere. That's what took me so long. Now, my dear, go to sleep, because we positively must leave in the morning.

MR. BROWN:

That is impossible.

MRS. BROWN:

We must go, my dear. I say that we must go. We must leave this hotel in the morning.

MR. BROWN:

Bother.

MRS. BROWN:

It's all very well for you to say that. But I say we must go tomorrow and we will.

MR. BROWN:

I do believe you want to kill me.

MRS. BROWN:

That is very cruel and most unjust. Nothing could be so bad for you as this wretched place where nobody can get warm either day or night. Only think how much more comfortable you will be at home. If we don't go, Uncle John will disown us.

MR. BROWN:

I don't believe a word of it.

BLACKOUT

SCENE III

The same. It is now morning and the Browns are preparing to leave. There is a knock on the door.

MRS. BROWN:

(opening the door) Yes?

BELLBOY:

Is this Madame's handkerchief?

MRS. BROWN:

Yes, it is mine. Here, take it Charles and come on.

MR. BROWN:

(very suspicious) What does this all mean?

BELLBOY:

A gentleman has been— Ah, er, something has been done to a gentleman.

MR. BROWN:

Something done to a gentleman?

BELLBOY:

Something very bad indeed.

MRS. BROWN:

(eager to stop this) Charles! We shall miss the train.

MR. BROWN:

What the mischief does it all mean?

MRS. BROWN:

What is the matter with you?

MR. BROWN:

What does it all mean? Did you go into somebody's room?

MRS. BROWN:

I did. Give me my handkerchief.

BELLBOY:

No.

MRS. BROWN:

Charles, we cannot allow ourselves to be delayed. Tonight is Christmas Eve and we shall not be at Thompson Hall. Think of my sister.

MR. BROWN:

But why did you go into some man's bedroom, my dear?

BELLBOY:

Yes, why?

MRS. BROWN:

It was a mistake, Charles. There is not a moment to lose. I will explain it all to you on the way.

BELLBOY:

But what is to be said to the gentleman?

MRS. BROWN:

You are not angry with me because I was in a man's room? What harm has been done, Charles? The man won't die because he's had a mustard plaster on his throat. (Jones enters) This has been a very disagreeable accident, Mr. Jones.

MR. JONES:

Accident! I don't know how it could have been an accident. This is a monstrous invasion of my privacy and personal comfort.

MR. BROWN:

Er, quite so, Mr. Jones. But on the part of the lady who is my wife—

MR. JONES:

So I understand. But the fact is, she did do it!

MR. BROWN:

She thought it was me!

MR. JONES:

What!

MR. BROWN:

My word as a gentleman. I have a bad sore throat, as you may perceive. And I asked my wife to get one for me. Just what she put on you.

MR. JONES:

I wish you had it!

MR. BROWN:

I wish so, too. I don't know when she will get over the shock.

MR. JONES:

I don't know when I shall! Why did she come into my room at all?

MR. BROWN:

She mistook the number.

MR. JONES:

She found out her mistake at least.

MR. BROWN:

Oh, yes.

MR. JONES:

Why didn't she wake me and take the damn thing off again?

MRS. BROWN:

Ah!

MR. JONES:

She can't have any human compassion in her heart.

MR. BROWN:

Ah! There was the difficulty.

MR. JONES:

Difficulty! Who was it had done it? To make a mistake like that and then leave it there and say nothing. It seems to me like a practical joke.

MR. BROWN:

No, Mr. Jones.

MR. JONES:

That's the way I look at it.

MR. BROWN:

There isn't a woman in all England less likely to play such a joke. If you're married yourself—

MR. JONES:

My wife would have wakened the man afterward. I'm sure she would. Why, she could have sent you if she was afraid to come herself. The whole thing is impossible.

CURTAIN

FROGGY

CAST OF CHARACTERS

The King

The Princess

The Frog

The Wizard

The Dowager

SCENE I

The Princess enters. She is a fully-grown and voluptuous woman, but she is dressed like a child in pigtails and a little child's dress. She has a big ball and a rattle and is playing with them by the pond. She comes in crying.

Princess

Wah, wah! Wah, wah!

Froggy

What's the matter, yer Highness?

Princess

I lost my pacifier. Wah.

Froggy (cagily)

Would ya like me to get if for ya, yer Majesty?

Princess (stops crying)

Would you do that? Oh, you sweet, darling frog. Lovey, lovey, lovey.

Froggy

I might do it.

Princess

Oh, please, please, sweet little Froggy.

Froggy

It wouldn't be easy, you know.

Princess

Please, sweet little Froggy. I can't stand it without my pacifier.

Froggy

OK, I'll do it for you, kid.

Princess

Lov'em's.

Froggy

I wouldn't do it for just anybody.

Princess

But you'll do it for me, sweet Froggy.

Froggy

But, what would you do for me?

Princess

Oh, I'll give you a kiss.

Froggy

Not enough!

Princess

Why not enough? What are you after, buster?

Froggy

Suppose I want money?

Princess

I'll give you all the gold your little heart ever pined for.

Froggy

Nah! I don't want gold.

Princess

Then, what do you want, power? I'll tell Daddy to make you prime minister.

Froggy

Would the King do that?

Princess

Daddy will do anything I tell him.

Froggy

Scout's honor?

Princess

Scout's honor.

Froggy

No. That's not what I want. I'll get your pacifier for you, but only if I can come to dinner with you tonight and sleep in your bed.

Princess

You dirty little green thing. I knew it. I knew it. All you frogs want the same thing from a Princess.

Froggy

If you are going to get abusive—

Princess

Frogs are all alike.

Froggy

Take it or leave it.

Princess

Wouldn't you rather have a big swimming pool or something, or a harem of females?

Froggy

Dinner and bed.

Princess

You frogs always drive such hard bargains. God, it's hard to be a Princess. Are you enchanted or something?

Froggy

I won't answer that question. You pays your penny and you takes your chances.

Princess

But, if you were a Prince or something, it would be so romantic.

Froggy

I regard this as strictly a business proposition.

Princess

Well, all right, I'll do it. But Daddy's not going to like it.

Froggy

Why not? It's happened in some of the best kingdoms.

Princess

Well, you see, Daddy wants to marry me to some sniveling little Prince or something dreadful like that, and he's invited just about everybody. He's trying to start a contest for my hand. The trouble is, they're all wimps. So well brought up, you know, and barely out of diapers.

Froggy

My presence will cause a sensation, if nothing else.

Princess

You know, you're right. I'll do it.

Froggy

It's a deal.

(The Frog goes out and returns quickly with a huge pacifier which the Princess embraces and immediately begins lapping and kissing.)

Princess

Izzums safe. Izzums come back to Mommy. Naughty thing.

Froggy

Er—what time is dinner, yer Majesty?

Princess

Eight o'clock sharp. Don't dress.

BLACKOUT

SCENE II

A hallway in the Palace outside the Royal Dining Hall. The King, his crown askew, comes out, followed by the Royal Wizard, who looks frightened.

Wizard

But, your Majesty, it is not my fault.

King

I am going to revive the Royal Edict about sorcery. Its salutary provisions have been neglected too long.

Wizard (outraged)

That law hasn't been enforced in centuries.

King

It's about time it was respected. Simple rules are good rules. All witches and sorcerers are to be burned at the stake. Mind that! Burned at the stake!

Wizard

A product of the Dark Ages! I thought Your Majesty was more enlightened. Besides, there have always been exceptions for the Court Sorcerer. It is well known that all laws are subject to reasonable exceptions.

King

The law says "all sorcerers." I know where to start looking. Now, I don't like that little joke. We are not amused.

Wizard

I had nothing to do with it.

King

Well, who the hell did?

Wizard

Search me.

King

I counted everybody. It's not one of us.

Wizard

It must be the work of some witch or something.

King

Well, can't you change him back to whatever he was before? It's damned embarrassing having a frog show up to dinner when you're trying to start a contest for the hand of your only daughter. I mean, he ordered a plate of flies!

Wizard

I'll do my best. Shh! Cheese it! He's coming.

(Enter the frog with a huge cocktail glass. He is looking rather happy.)

Froggy

Evening, yer Majesty. Merry Christmas.

King

Good evening, my dear sir. Delighted to have you with us, my dear fellow. Did you enjoy your meal?

Froggy

Finest kind.

King

Cook had a little difficulty catching them, but I'll tell him you enjoyed it.

Froggy

Immensely.

(The Wizard is making passes around the Frog and endeavoring not to be noticed.)

Froggy

Here now, what are you trying to do, mate?

Wizard

Oh, just making a pass.

Froggy

What kind of frog do you think I am, anyway? You'd better keep an eye on this fellow, Yer Majeshtee. (gulps) Rivet. Oh, excuse me, I'm a little drunk.

King

It's too bad you're leaving so soon.

Froggy

I ain't leaving yet. Party ain't over.

King

Staying long?

Froggy

Overnight.

Princess (entering)

It's a friend of mine, Daddy. Can he stay the night? Can he? Can he?

King

Oh, all right. (aside to her) You do have a tendency to make undesirable acquaintances, my dear. Heaven only knows what common pond this frog came from. (aloud, sweetly) What was the promise, my dear?

Princess

To have him to dinner with us—

Dowager (entering)

Was that all?

Princess (innocently)

And to sleep the night in my bed.

Dowager

I knew it. Hanky-panky. That's all these young girls think of today. Hanky-panky.

Princess

I haven't done anything wrong. He saved my pacifier. And I love him, so there.

Dowager

You will explain your disgraceful behavior!

Princess

I will not. I can do what I want. I am the Princess.

Dowager

Are you going to just stand there and let her get away with it, you spineless wretch?

King

Now, look here, Sis, I'm the King and I can have your head chopped off.

Dowager

Just because you've got a pair of balls doesn't mean you've got any balls.

Froggy (to the Wizard)

Hands off, you overgrown fairy.

Dowager

The only reason you're King is that Father forgot to make his will. He was going to make me Queen because he knew I could govern.

King

Oh, shut up. You always were a pain in the ass!

Dowager

Well, I know my duty, even if you don't.

King

The Princess doesn't know. We never told her.

Dowager

Never told her!

King

Her mother didn't think it a proper story.

Dowager

It isn't a proper story. That's why everyone assumed she knew it. Girls are so sly these days.

Princess (jumping up and down)

Will someone please tell me what's wrong! It's only a frog. I'm sure he knows the proper thing to do in bed.

Dowager

Child! What are you saying? Wizard, did you laugh?

Wizard

I had a frog in my throat.

King

Now, cut that out. (to Princess) Your Aunt is referring to a family scandal. It happened once before. The frog turned into a prince—so you see how it is.

Princess

That's what they all do, isn't it? What's wrong with that?

King

Well, once the frog got in bed with her, he or it turned into a man. A REAL MAN! If you know what I mean. You see, it broke the spell.

Princess

But, that's what's supposed to happen. Sounds romantic.

Dowager

In my day we were at least modest.

King

Were you? Before my time, of course.

Dowager

That cough of yours is very troublesome, Wizard.

King

This is a terrible thing to happen.

Dowager

It hasn't happened yet, and what's more, it won't.

Princess

I still don't understand.

Froggy

Look, dummy, they're afraid I'll have sex with you.

Princess

Sex? Yummy, yummy. I always wanted to have SEX.

Dowager

You see! You see!

King

Honey, maybe Daddy will buy you a new toy instead. How would you like a big pacifier? Sugar-coated?

Princess

But, I've given my word. Did the Prince marry her?

Dowager (dolefully)

No. They just lived together.

Princess

Wow. I always wanted to live with somebody.

Dowager

You see what will happen if we don't protect the poor innocent.

Princess

If I can't take Froggy to bed, I'll cry.

King

Well, honey, if you really want to.

Princess

I do, I do.

Dowager

I see your Majesty is bent on condoning your daughter's lack of morals.

King

Watch it, Sis.

Dowager

Have you no sense of propriety at all? To take a strange Prince to bed with you, without even having been properly introduced—I call that lax.

King

A frog, Sis, a frog.

Dowager

You have no sense of history. If you did, you'd know that at the moment the spell is broken, the Prince awakes with a huge—

Princess

What a mind you've got, Auntie. You think of everything.

Dowager

I do. I shall sleep in your room tonight, Miss.

Princess

What do you want to do that for?

Dowager

I have the most pressing reasons. I know what men are.

Princess

Not very likely.

Dowager (pulling the Princess out)

Come, child.

Princess

Wah, wah.

(The Dowager and Princess exit.)

BLACKOUT

SCENE III

The bedroom of the Princess. The Dowager is present, looking in the mirror and preening like a swan.

Dowager

My figure is still good.

(Enter Frog.)

Frog

Evening, old lady. Happy New Year.

Dowager

Amphibious wretch.

Frog

Watch what you say there, mama.

Dowager

Peeping tadpole.

Frog

What's your game?

Dowager

I'll teach you.

Frog

Rivet. Help! She's crazy.

Dowager

Rapist! Intrude on a lady in her nightdress.

(The Dowager chases the frog, who jumps out of the window.)

Frog

Rivet. Rivet. AIIIEEE!

Dowager

If women would defend themselves the way I did, there wouldn't be any hanky-panky. A just reward for licentiousness.

(Enter Princess with her Teddy Bear.)

Princess

I'm sorry I'm late.

Dowager

Never mind, dear. Hurry up and get into bed.

Princess

Where's the frog? Did he come yet?

Dowager

He's not here.

Princess

I'd better call him.

Dowager

You'll do no such thing. A frog that can't turn up on time for bed doesn't deserve to get any—

(A knock on the door.)

Princess

Come in.

Dowager

No one can come in!

(The King enters, accompanied by a frog.)

King

Hang it, Sis, I'm her father.

Dowager

I've always doubted that. Your wife was a sly one. Who's that?

King

The Frog, of course. Who does it look like? We've been getting on beautifully. He's got a priceless story about a traveling knight and a peasant's daughter.

Dowager

It!

King

It then! He was looking cold, so I—

Dowager

Really, Your Majesty!

Princess

He'll be snug here. I'll keep you warm, Froggy, I mean your Highness.

Dowager

Well, I never.

King

I'll just look in during the night. I'd like to know as soon as our distinguished guest is himself again.

Dowager

Spending the night with strange frogs. Modern girls!

BLACKOUT

SCENE IV

Another room in the King's palace. The King is alone and looks rather disheveled. The Princess invades the room. She no longer has her pacifier and her hair is not longer in pigtails. She looks her age.

Princess

Daddy, daddy, daddy—where is he?

King

Who?

Princess

The Frog Prince. I had the most glorious dream about him. I dreamed he took off all my clothes and then he—

King

Most extraordinary about that frog.

Princess

I just want to kiss him and kiss him and kiss him. I woke up and he was gone.

King

Such a lot of fuss about nothing. Really, your Aunt—

Princess

I know, I know. But what has happened?

King

The contest is off, of course.

Princess

Father, tell me where he is. I'm going crazy.

King

Bless me, don't you know?

Princess

Oh, I fell asleep and I dreamed the most beautiful hunk was making love to me. But I woke up in a sweat and no one was there. Wah. Wah.

King

Well, about four o'clock this morning, the spell was broken and the Frog assumed human form. And what a form.

Princess

Where is he? (jumping up and down) I want him now. I want him now. Is he sinful? Are we going to have a scandal?

King

Well, yes, there's going to be a scandal.

Princess

Whee! Auntie will be so pleased.

King

You see, the Frog was not a prince after all.

Princess

Huh? He wasn't a peasant, was he?

King

Oh, no.

Princess

Then, I don't care. I want him anyway.

King

Well, you can't have him. It was a Princess.

Princess

A Princess?

King

The loveliest Princess you ever did see. Auntie doesn't like her, but you will. You'll love her.

Princess

I don't think I'm going to like her at all. I want a hunk. Where is she?

King

She's—er—in my bed.

Princess

Father!

King

Yes, dear. I've been thinking about getting you a new

mother for some time now. Wouldn't you like to have a new mother?

Princess

No little bitch is going to scheme her way into this family by pretending to be a frog and worming her way into your bed by getting in bed with me!

King

You will not talk that way about your stepmother.

Princess

Stepmother! Over my dead body!

King

If you like. Don't forget I'm King and what I say goes.

Princess

Daddy!

King

But you'll like her. She knows the very latest racy stories. And she knows all the new troubadours— every one, intimately. She'll be more like a sister than a mother to you.

Woman's Voice

Darling, won't you hurry up?

King (straightening his crown)

Duty calls. Coming, my dear.

(Exit the King to his bedroom.)

Princess

Would you believe that!

(Enter Frog.)

Frog

Rivet.

Princess

Can't you keep your shape for one minute, Princess?

Frog

I ain't no Princess, I'm a Prince.

Princess

Really? You're sure?

Frog

'Course I'm sure. It's me, Prince Floriman, don't you recognize me?

Princess

You don't look like yourself. But, what are you doing like that?

Frog

Well, the Wizard laid this spell on me. He couldn't change the other frog back, so he tried changing me to a frog, too, and then he couldn't change me back. Stupidest sorcerer I've ever met.

Princess

Then, it wasn't you last night?

Frog

Certainly not. I went to your room, but before you got there, your Aunt chased me out. She is one daffy bitch. Pushed me out the window. A wonder I didn't kill myself.

Princess

You poor thing. But, you can't stay like this.

Frog

I not only can, but will, until the spell is broken.

Princess

How can that be done?

Frog

The idea is the same.

Princess

Why, you little devil, you…you mean?

Frog

Bed and dinner.

Princess

We dine at eight. Don't dress.

(The Princess and the Frog go out together. The Dowager comes in and glowers at them.)

Dowager

Now she's got another one. I told him if they have one, they always want more. I told him.

CURTAIN

THE GOLDEN GOBLIN

CAST OF CHARACTERS

KELCH

FILINA

HOCHY

FILINA'S FATHER

THE OWL

THE GOLDEN GOBLIN

SHADOWS

SCENE I

Filina's father's house.

FATHER:

You marry my daughter? What an idea! You haven't any money.

KELCH:

But I can give her love. And that is much better than money.

FATHER:

I don't think so. Anyone can make love. But few can make money. So go back to your woodcutting and don't come to me with such silly requests.

KELCH:

Is there no chance for me?

FATHER:

Yes, there's one. Become as rich as Hochy and you shall marry my daughter.

BLACKOUT

SCENE II

The woods.

FIRST ELF:

Who is this youth lying asleep?

SECOND ELF:

His name's Kelch and he loves Filina who is about to marry old Hochy. He's now searching for the castle of The Wicked Baron to ask for gold.

FIRST ELF:

He'll never find the castle unless he asks the owl who lives in the oak tree that he's sleeping under.

KELCH:

(waking) Thanks for the advice. I'll ask her. (the Elves run off)

Foxy owl

Clever fowl

Please tell me

Where to see

Where Baron Bold

Hoards up his gold.

OWL:

(above in the tree) Go away, boy. Do not disturb my grief. The Baron is dead and I am mourning for him.

KELCH:

The Baron is dead! Oh, dear. Then I won't be able to get any gold. Still, he cannot have taken his gold with him. So it must be there still.

Owl, owl

Midnight's fowl

Where's the castle?

OWL:

Stand up, look around

Jump around.

Turn around.

Wander, wander

Yonder, yonder.

Look ahead.

KELCH:

(follows the instructions and the castle appears)

OWL:

Through lovely hills

The moonlight falls

There you will find

The Goblin golden

Who, since ages olden

Has ruled mankind.

Another victim

He will find.

BLACKOUT

SCENE III

The goblin's castle.

GOBLIN:

(sitting on a pile of gold) I know what you've come for, so take as much gold as you like—and go!

KELCH:

But where is the Wicked Baron?

GOBLIN:

He is my servant now.

KELCH:

Can I take some gold?

GOBLIN:

Sure. As much as you like.

KELCH:

Really?

GOBLIN:

Sure. There's plenty more where this came from.

KELCH:

I don't have to sign my name in blood or something?

GOBLIN:

You've been listening to too many fairy tales.

KELCH:

Thanks. (begins filling his pockets)

GOBLIN:

May I ask why you want gold? You don't look like the type that usually comes here?

KELCH:

Have you heard of Filina?

GOBLIN:

Filina? Oh, yes. The most beautiful girl in the whole kingdom! Who hasn't heard of her?

KELCH:

(gesturing) I want this so I can marry her.

GOBLIN:

Ah! Well, here. Take this ring and put it on her finger as a wedding present from me.

KELCH:

Thank you kindly. It will do for a wedding ring.

GOBLIN:

Exactly. It will do perfectly for a wedding ring. Now fill your pockets with gold and that will do for Filina's dowry.

KELCH:

But I really shouldn't take this. It belongs to the Wicked Baron.

GOBLIN:

No, it doesn't. The Wicked Baron's dead and his gold belongs to whomever I choose to give it. All the gold in the world is mine. Take as much as you like. Need a bag? Let it never be said I am not generous.

KELCH:

Thank you! Thank you!

GOBLIN:

Now, off with you. Goodbye. Till I see you again.

KELCH:

You'll never see me again. I'm not greedy.

GOBLIN:

Oh yes I will, Now don't forget to marry Filina with my ring.

KELCH:

I won't forget. Bless you.

GOBLIN:

Bye, bye. (aside) Sucker!

BLACKOUT

SCENE IV

The forest.

OWL:

(spying Kelch, who enters cheerfully with gold) Oh, you've come back.

KELCH:

Yes, and I've got the gold, thanks to you.

OWL:

Much good it may do you.

KELCH:

What a rude fowl.

BLACKOUT

SCENE V

The forest.

OWL:

To Whit! To Whoo!

KELCH:

True wit I have not. Owing to my sorrow. And I go not to woo because Filina has been taken from me.

OWL:

Why do you sit under my tree and cry?

KELCH:

Because I'm so miserable.

OWL:

What! Did you lose your gold?

KELCH:

No. I took the gold to Filina's father and he agreed to the marriage.

OWL:

Well then?

KELCH:

But, when I placed the ring the goblin gave me on Filina's finger— (weeps)

OWL:

Well, young man?

KELCH:

She vanished.

OWL:

Ah, that Goblin. I know him well. He carried off my friend the Wicked Baron, who was no more wicked than you except that he was too fond of gold. That was his ruin. If it had not been for his love of gold, the Goblin would not have carried him off.

KELCH:

Why did he carry the Wicked Baron off?

OWL:

Once a year the Golden Goblin makes a human sacrifice to the King of Fire.

KELCH:

Why?

OWL:

So the King of Fire won't invade the Realm of Gold and melt the Goblin's domain. He offered the Baron as the last victim. The next will be Filina!

KELCH:

Filina! Oh, no. It cannot be true.

OWL:

It is true, quite true. The ring he gave you is a magic ring. As soon as it was placed on Filina's finger, she vanished from the earth.

KELCH:

It's true, it's true. She did. But where is she now?

OWL:

Down below in the Realm of Gold. Tomorrow she will be given up as the Bride of the King of Fire.

KELCH:

I've got to save her. What can I do?

OWL:

I don't know. If your heart is strong and you aren't afraid, there's a chance.

KELCH:

Oh, I'm not afraid. Do help me save her, dear Mr. Owl, please do!

OWL:

I'll help you. On one condition. And that is that you never cut down my oak tree and never let anyone else do it.

KELCH:

I swear to you that your oak tree will always be safe.

OWL:

Then we've got a deal. Now first you must go to the

Realm of Gold.

KELCH:

How?

OWL:

Keep your hair on and I'll tell you. The way is concealed in the trunk of this tree. Now take this phial of water.

KELCH:

What good will it do?

OWL:

A great deal of good! All the subjects of the Golden Goblin are mortals who are distracted by gold. That water is the water of contentment. If you touch anyone with it, his lust for gold is forgotten and he becomes satisfied with his station in life.

KELCH:

Is such a thing possible?

OWL:

Didn't I just tell you?

KELCH:

But how will it help me?

OWL:

Why, the Goblin will lose all his subjects. When he sees that, trust me, he'll make a deal quick.

KELCH:

But how do humans get into the Realm of Gold?

OWL:

They go in their dreams. When awake, they live on earth, but at night, in their dreams, they are the slaves of the Goblin. Indeed, many of them are his slaves during the day as well as at night. Now get going or you'll be too late.

KELCH:

Thanks, I'm off. (enters the tree)

OWL:

There's no doubt about it. I'm a wise old owl. I've saved my tree, rescued Filina, and revenged my friend the Wicked Baron. What will I do for my next trick? Beats me.

BLACKOUT

SCENE VI

The Realm of Gold. People are picking up nuggets of gold and stuffing them in their pockets. But the bottoms of the pockets are cut off so they must constantly be refilled. No one pays any attention to the other. Each has a dazed expression. Some have chains and necklaces of gold. Kelch arrives and observes. Then he sprays water on them from an atomizer like perfume. As he does so, each person ceases to be interested in gold and leaves nonchalantly. The Golden Goblin rushes in with his guards.

GOBLIN:

Just what do you think you are doing? Are you trying to rob me of my subjects? I'm going to give you to the King of Fire! Seize him!

KELCH:

(as the guards rush him, Kelch sprays them with water; they stop, look confused, and leave) So much for your guards.

GOBLIN:

(stamping in rage) You stay away from me! Don't come near me with that stuff! What is it anyway? And what do you want? You are disrupting the order of the universe, young man. What do you want?

KELCH:

Stuff it! You know quite well what I want. I want Filina. You stole my Filina from me.

GOBLIN:

I stole her fair and square. She's mine now. And you were well paid for her. You took a lot of gold.

KELCH:

You said it was a present.

GOBLIN:

If you'll believe that, you'll believe anything. No one gives gold for nothing. Don't be a fool.

KELCH:

You tricked me. I never said you could steal my future wife. I want Filina and not your gold.

GOBLIN:

Is that so? Well I don't believe you. You are the first human I've ever heard say that.

KELCH:

We're wasting time. If you don't give me back Filina, I am going to take away all your subjects. And you can be all alone with your gold.

GOBLIN:

Wait! Wait! Let's talk. Don't do anything foolish. Suppose I give you back your Filina?

KELCH:

Let's suppose that if you don't, I— (gestures with his atomizer)

GOBLIN:

Let's talk this over. How about a drink?

KELCH:

No thanks. Looks yucky.

GOBLIN:

Damn you, kid. You're a tough one. Suppose I give you

back Filina? On conditions.

KELCH:

I'm going to make some conditions of my own.

GOBLIN:

Stop! Stop! Sure I can't interest you in a drink?

KELCH:

I said no!

GOBLIN:

You're a smart kid. If you'd drunk that stuff, you'd have turned into a statue. Like that one.

KELCH:

(looking at the statue) Hey! That's Filina.

GOBLIN:

You still want her?

KELCH:

I can't take my Filina back like this.

GOBLIN:

So, don't be unreasonable. She's no good to you like that, and she's far too valuable as a statue for me to give her to you. Let's make a deal.

KELCH:

(obstinately) Filina is more valuable than a statue.

GOBLIN:

More valuable than a solid gold statue? You've got to be kidding.

KELCH:

I'm not kidding.

GOBLIN:

You expect me to believe you'd rather have a woman made of flesh and blood rather than all this gold?

KELCH:

Yes. That's exactly what I expect you to believe.

GOBLIN:

I wasn't born yesterday. (Kelch starts to gesture threateningly with his atomizer) Okay, okay. You're a strange kid. My magic doesn't work with you. But you got to look at it from my point of view.

KELCH:

What exactly is your point of view?

GOBLIN:

If I give you back Filina, then I have a problem.

KELCH:

What problem?

GOBLIN:

The thing is: how do I pay my annual tribute to the King of Fire? See, I'd like to help you, but— (gestures helplessly)

KELCH:

Find a substitute.

GOBLIN:

A substitute?

KELCH:

Yeah. (spelling it out) S-U-B-S-T-I-T-U-T-E.

GOBLIN:

Okay. Where do I get one?

KELCH:

Suppose I bring you Hochy? He weighs a lot more than Filina.

GOBLIN:

(after walking up and down, gesturing to himself, thinking about it) Okay, bring me Hochy and I'll give you Filina.

KELCH:

What will you do to him?

GOBLIN:

I'll give him to the King of Fire.

KELCH:

He'll be burned up.

GOBLIN:

Nah! Scorched a little. Just the bad part.

KELCH:

Only the bad part?

GOBLIN:

Yeah. Trust me.

KELCH:

In that case there won't be anything left.

GOBLIN:

There's good in everybody. Look on it as if you are doing him a favor.

KELCH:

A favor?

GOBLIN:

You bet. Sure. Everybody should be purified. Doesn't every religion provide for it? If Hochy goes on at the rate he's going, there won't be enough time left in infinity for him to get out of Purgatory.

KELCH:

Anyway, I don't see why I should care about Hochy. I hate him. He wants to marry Filina.

GOBLIN:

Deal?

KELCH:

Deal.

GOBLIN:

Now, here's what you must do. Take Filina back with you as she is. Get this Hochy character to pull off the ring that's on her wedding finger and put it on his own.

KELCH:

Then what?

GOBLIN:

Filina will be her old self.

KELCH:

And Hochy?

GOBLIN:

Hochy will be enjoying my company.

KELCH

No tricks.

GOBLIN:

No tricks. Word of a Prince.

(Kelch struggles to lift the statue of Filina, but she's too heavy. He winds up dragging her rather than carrying her off.)

BLACKOUT

SCENE VII

Kelch's cottage.

Kelch, puffing, drags in Filina's statue. Her Father, Hochy, and townsfolk are present.

HOCHY:

Here's the wicked magician.

FATHER:

He robbed me of my daughter.

KELCH:

I've brought her back. Behold!

FATHER:

(inspecting the statue) It's my daughter sure enough. But she's changed into gold.

KELCH:

Would you rather have your daughter alive or a Golden Statue?

HOCHY

(pulling Filina's father by the sleeve, whispering) Say, the Golden Statue.

FATHER:

No, no! (sententiously) No gold can recompense me for the loss of my daughter.

HOCHY:

But your daughter is going to marry me.

FATHER:

That's true enough.

HOCHY:

Well consider my preferences. I would rather have her as a golden statue. I always said she was worth her weight in gold and now she is.

KELCH:

You hear what he says! I love Filina for herself. Hochy

loves her for her gold. He'd rather have her as a golden statue than as a real live woman. Wretch!

HOCHY:

She's mine! (standing in front of the statue possessively) I have her father's word and all this gold is my own.

FATHER:

(worried) What will you do with her?

HOCHY:

Melt her down immediately. Into the furnace she goes.

FATHER:

What! Melt my daughter! Never! You shall not have her. I'll give her to Kelch.

KELCH:

Keep your word and I'll change her into a living woman once more.

FATHER:

Give me back my daughter and you will be her husband,

HOCHY:

No, no. The statue, I mean Filina, is my wife. Mine.

KELCH:

(to Father) What do you say?

FATHER:

You shall be her husband.

HOCHY:

If you give him the golden stat—I mean Filina—I'll ruin you and the whole village. You know I can do it.

KELCH:

I'll bring back Filina and I'll get rid of Hochy.

HOCHY:

Did you hear that? A threat! He intends to murder me!

(Hochy hides behind the statue,)

KELCH:

I'm not making any threats at all.

HOCHY:

Then I'd like to know how you will get rid of me. (clinging to the statue)

KELCH:

I'll buy you off.

HOCHY:

I love the stat— I mean Filina, I can't be bought off.

KELCH:

I'll give you more gold than you ever saw in your life.

HOCHY:

More than Filina?

KELCH:

Yes. Will you agree to that?

KELCH:

Betcha.

HOCHY:

You're on. Now what?

KELCH:

Just pull that ring off Filina's finger.

HOCHY:

(pulling off the ring.) Ring's off. Now what?

KELCH:

Place it on your finger.

HOCHY:

What's the good of that?

KELCH:

Just follow instructions.

HOCHY:

To humor you. Let's get it over with.

(There's a puff of smoke and blinding flash of light. When the smoke clears, Hochy has disappeared and Filina has materialized as a beautiful young girl.)

ALL:

Where's Hochy?

KELCH:

Gone where he won't trouble us again. Now, I marry Filina.

ALL:

Yes. Yes.

(A wedding dance begins and all the characters dance.)

CURTAIN

REHEARSING
DON QUIXOTE
A SKIT FOR CHILDREN

CAST OF CHARACTERS

THE TEACHER

FIRST BOY

SECOND BOY

THIRD BOY

LITTLE GIRL

SECOND GIRL

FAT BOY

STUDIOUS OLDER CHILD

CARMEN

MACHO BOY

PEDRO

JUAN

THE PLAY

A school room for children between ages 6 and 10.

TEACHER

Now children, I told you we were preparing a treat for you. Today we're going to celebrate Don Quixote de la Mancha, and we're going to put on a play about him.

1st. BOY

I want to be Don Quixote!

2nd BOY

You're too fat. I will play Don Quixote.

3rd BOY

No, me.

1st BOY

My Daddy's tougher than your Daddy!

2nd BOY

So what? I'm tougher than you.

TEACHER

Children children—behave! I will pick Don Quixote.

THE CHILDREN

Yes, teacher!

LITTLE GIRL

Is someone going to play Dulcinea?

TEACHER (nodding)

Yes.

2nd GIRL

Me! Me!

1st GIRL

You're too ugly.

3rd GIRL

And you're too fat.

TEACHER

STOP! STOP! This is horrible. If you don't stop fighting there'll be no play.

CHILDREN

Yes, teacher.

FAT BOY (timidly)

If there's a part for Sancho Panza, I'd like to try out for it.

BOYS

Go for it, Fatso! You're a natural. We don't want to be Sancho—it's all yours.

ANOTHER BOY

What about the horse?

TEACHER

The horse? I hadn't thought of the horse.

SEVERAL CHILDREN

We want to play Don Quixote's horse.

TEACHER

I'd have to write the part. Okay, I can do that.

LITTLE GIRL

Can the horse talk?

TEACHER

Sure.

CHILDREN

What about his dog?

TEACHER

He didn't have a dog.

SEVERAL CHILDREN

It would be nice if he had a dog. Let's give him a dog.

TEACHER

Why not? What shall we call the dog?

BOY

I have a dog named Bono. Let's call him Bono.

ALL

Bono it is.

STUDIOUS OLDER BOY or GIRL

And the windmill? I want to play the windmill.

CHILDREN

He's crazy. Nobody can play a windmill.

STUDIOUS BOY/GIRL

I can, too.

(He waves his arms)

ALL (including the Teacher)

Ha, ha, ha.

TEACHER

(handing out papers)

Here are some lines I want you to read from the skit I've written. Who wants to read first?

CARMEN

I do!

TEACHER

But this is Don Quixote's part.

BOYS

Boo, Carmen!

TEACHER

I'm going to let the boys read first.

CARMEN (furious)

Sexist!

(crying)

It's not fair. I'm as good as any boy here.

CHILDREN

Crybaby feminist!

TEACHER

Pedro—will you read?

PEDRO

Sure.

(he starts to read but stops)

(pompously)

I cannot read while that child is crying!

(Carmen stops crying and begins to plot Pedro's death)

(Pedro reads his lines)

(The children applaud)

TEACHER

Thank you, Pedro.

(to another boy)

Juan?

JUAN

(very shy)

I can't.

TEACHER

Come on, try.

JUAN

(reads haltingly)

TEACHER

Thanks: you did just fine.

(several more boys read)

(after all the boys read)

Now you, Carmen.

CARMEN

No, I don't want to.

CHILDREN

Go ahead, Carmen.

TEACHER (coaxingly)

Come on, Carmen.

CARMEN

(reads very well)

TEACHER

You'd make a great Don Quixote!

CARMEN

See, everybody!!

TEACHER

Now, let's read Dulcinea.

MACHO BOY

I'd like to read that part.

ALL

You, Rodrigo.

(all laugh)

MACHO BOY

What's so funny? I'll kick all your asses. Anyway, I was just kidding.

(all laugh)

BOY

I want to be Bono—woof, woof.

ANOTHER BOY

No, me.

CHILDREN

Woof! Woof!

(They start fighting)

TEACHER

This is too much. I cannot go on! The play is canceled!

(The Teacher begins to cry in a nervous breakdown)

Why did I ever want to teach!

CURTAIN

ROBERT THE DEVIL

CAST OF CHARACTERS

The Duke of Normandy

The Duchess of Normandy

The Devil

Satan

Two Hermits

The Nurse

Robert the Devil

Two Barons

The Squire

Third Hermit

A Water Carrier

The Emperor of Rome

The Seneschal

The Constable

The Angel

The Princess

Confidant of the Princess

A Knight

SCENE I
PROLOGUE

Duke

Ha, Madame, m'love, why is it I always have to find you in your oratory? You're crying? It's not tears the Duke of Normandy wants from his wife, but children.

Duchess

Sire, my spouse, pity! Each day your reproaches assail me and wound me profoundly. Are they pursuing me even to this chair where I seek refuge and kneel to pray to God?

Duke

Who doesn't grant us a son for all your praying.

Duchess

Is that my fault?

Duke

Is it mine, Madame? By my faith, if I didn't respect in you the daughter of a noble lineage, I could tell you what I did in my youth, which gives me confidence and the right to insist on an heir from you.

Duchess

Sire, my friend, haven't I always performed all my duty?

Duke

Your duty was not to remain barren after seventeen years of marriage. I am enraged when I see the most humble of my servants encumbered with jugs full of children while I grow old without a son to inherit my duchy. If you were to ask your God to render me a widower, that at least would give me a chance.

(Exit Duke.)

Duchess (alone)

He's gone—cursing me again from his mouth and in his heart. Each day for seventeen years his reproaches have assailed me, and each day they grow more cruel! I am desperate. I pray in vain for heaven to give me a son! And heaven remains deaf. And you, devil in hell, if I were to ask you—would you remain deaf as well? What did I say? Angels of God, save me! My women, come. Don't leave me alone! Wretch! It's I who insisted on solitude when I pray. I'm afraid! Night has fallen. What beast, invisible and gross, crawls in the shadow at the foot of the wall, beating its wings around me? Ah, mercy! I am fainting.

SCENE II

In Hell.

Satan

Devil? Did you hear?

Devil

I heard, Lord Satan.

Satan

You took note?

Devil

Everything is noted.

Satan

Ha, ha! You never call the devil in vain, souls at bay. The vow of the Duchess of Normandy is inscribed on the pages of the book of Hell.

SCENE III

Twenty years after. Before the Château d'Argues. Several hermits and Robert's nurse.

Hermit

Come, my brothers. Let's pursue our way. Ah, still those shouts, those whimperings, those fires! Merciful God, save us!

Nurse

I'm going there myself. It's up there. See, the ramparts, its fourteen towers, its dungeon, and the window from which my good mistress the Duchess of Normandy peers. What do you want, good hermits?

Hermit

Alas, good lady, we have all seven of us left our hermitage in the forest. For the forest near here is full of poor people in flight. We are seeking bread and aid for them. Mercy on us. On that hill, look! Another monastery burning.

Nurse

Robert the Devil has passed by here.

Hermit

Is it possible he can be the son of the Duke of Normandy?

Nurse

As for me, I rather think he's the son of the devil, though twenty years ago I was one of his nurses. Hardly had he been born than he tore up, with his nails and his teeth, the breasts of his nurses, and we had to suckle him through an ivory horn. From the time he walked, he tortured animals, wounded grievously his little comrades, disemboweled the dogs of the Duke, his father. Young man, handsome as an archangel, but crueler than a demon from hell, he left the Château and placed himself at the head of a band of damned men to pillage the whole country. But I hear a cavalcade coming on the road. Flee, good hermits! As for me, I'm running to the Château. There's going to be another battle. Eh! No, they are friends of Milord the Duke.

(Trumpets sound.)

Herald

Oyez! By the order of the Duke of Normandy, it is decreed and proclaimed that, for their crimes, Robert the Devil and his accomplices are to be pursued and hounded. That, by field and forest, all faithful render assistance.

(Sound of trumpets. Robert the Devil appears.)

Robert

Robert the Devil? Here he is! Hello? They're going already. I've come too late with my mercenaries. That's a shame! But, by God's head, if Milord, my father, wants to ban me from my inheritance, it wasn't worth the trouble, perhaps, to teach me how to mount a horse! And, if he thinks, by granting me Knighthood, to teach me wisdom, he is badly mistaken. Hola! Who are those two that are coming towards me? And why have my good lads let them pass through alive?

Two Barons

Sir Robert, listen.

Robert

I listen when I feel like it. Who are you?

Barons

Two Barons of the Duke your father. He says unto you: "I wanted nothing more than a son. I have one. But he is such that I would be relieved if he were to die before my eyes. He must leave!"

Robert

Before my eyes? Ha! Ha! Hey there, my soldiers, my gallows birds, my executioners. Take these two Barons of my father! Put out their right eyes.

Barons

Sir Robert, son of our Lord, pity, by Jesus Christ!

Robert

Shut up, stupid. With one eye the less you can follow my tracks. It's everywhere marked by villages destroyed, by convents aflame, by nuns weeping for all their treasures, and not just those of their chapels. Ah! My respected father finds me bad? Very well! I will be worse.

(Robert's accomplices lead away the Barons and put out their eyes. The Barons scream.)

Robert

Who are those still over there? Who put you in a bunch here, pale faces?

(The Hermits reappear.)

Hermit

Sir, we are seven hermits who pray to God, night and

day.

Robert

Oh, really? Well, I am going to send you to rejoin him in heaven, and tell him how I sharpened my sword which is blunt on your necks. Hey-ho! There's one dead. How easy he fell. How his head bounces down the road. I'm a good bowler. Hey-ho, here's two, three—

(The other Hermits kneel.)

Hermits

All powerful God, pardon him!

Robert

And four—and five. Come on, show your neck—you there. And seven. Seven heads fallen! Now that I've taken the matter in hand, forward, my men! These destitute hermits had only their bows. But here, over there, a rich convent where we will measure out jewels and gold by the bushel. To saddle, my Squire! What, you lower your eyes? You are counting the heads? There are seven, my lad. I give them to you. No? You don't budge? What is it, my loyal one? I've never seen you this way.

Squire

Milord, these men were living in poverty and holiness.

I cannot judge my master, but I feel shame and horror! Kill me, too, if you like.

Robert

Why do you tell me that, you who've held my saddle when I depart for all my crimes? I, too, suddenly, as if a luminous dart pierced me, I ask myself why I am without respite, assailed by this taste for evil, for blood, for murder. Who am I then? Why do they call me Robert the Devil? I swear by these innocent bodies which lie there, that today I will have the truth. I am going to ask my mother, in her castle. To horse!

(Bells tolling in the distance.)

BLACKOUT

SCENE IV

The Duchess of Normandy, a black veil over her white hair, sits beside a high window in the dungeon. Near her, spinning, the Nurse.

Nurse

Then, our good lady, I saw him near the castle, as he went to commit new crimes, and as he turned to ridicule the edict proclaimed by the heralds of our Lord, the Duke, his father. Heart beating fast, I crossed over the drawbridge and returned to the Château to give the alarm. Your son, at the head of his band of which he is the dreaded chief, is burning villages, torturing peasants, stopping and killing travelers, pillaging and burning monasteries, himself strangling the holy nuns and returning, always, gorged with plunder, blood, and infamy to his terrible lair in the depths of the forest. Neither tears, nor prayers, nor penitence have succeeded in appeasing the wrath of heaven. The infernal curse weighs heavily on Robert the Devil!

Duchess

The infernal curse weighs on the son of my flesh. But, listen, nurse! Those shouts?

Nurse

I am afraid, noble lady.

(Shouts can be heard.)

Duchess

Listen! What new misfortune befalls us? Those terrified shouts of servants on the stairs, that flight throughout the castle! That clash of halberds of our men at arms! Good heavens! It's him! It's my son!

Nurse

Oh, dear lady! He's here. Clothed in mail, covered with blood. Robert, your son, his naked sword in hand.

(Robert the Devil enters, terrible. The nurse falls to her knees. The mother stands erect, arms crossed, but wanting to flee.)

Robert

Mother, don't flee! And, don't add to the weight of my crimes the horror of seeing my own mother fleeing from me like an outcast.

Duchess

My son, mercy for these poor people.

Robert

I have not struck anyone in the house of my mother.

Duchess

Your clothes are drenched in blood!

Robert

That blood doesn't come from here. But, I want to know what curse weighs on me. Am I the son of the devil? Speak!

Duchess

Wretched child! Let the curse of which you are the victim fall back on me! It is I who brought the sin. Son! Cut off my head! Do justice!

Robert

Mother, I bend my knee and beg you. A man who's done what I've done can hear anything.

Duchess

My son, for a word that escaped me in a moment of

sorrow, of madness, I vowed you, without knowing it, without wishing it, to the infernal powers. Today is the first day, since your birth, that I can speak to you as to a human being. Must God then have pity on us?

Robert

I don't know, mother. My soul is caked and hardened with innocent blood. I cannot even ask your forgiveness. But, ever since my sword cut the throat of seven hermits, a voice within me speaks against me, and reproaches me for my crimes. I begin to understand the horror I inspire. Only the Pope, if he would listen to my confession, could absolve me. I am leaving for Rome. Pray for me.

(Exit Robert the Devil.)

Nurse

He's going away, Madame Duchess.

Duchess

Ah, beautiful returned son, I am losing you already. But, lean out the window, Nurse. What are those new shouts?

Nurse (looking out the window)

It's your son Robert, who's killing all the brigands, his companions who were waiting for him outside the castle.

Duchess

Are we at the end of our trials? And, must his repentance, like his crimes, be stained with blood?

BLACKOUT

SCENE V

The hut of penitence.

Squire

It's indeed here, Milord.

Robert

Squire, call me Robert. I am a penitent dressed as a pilgrim.

Squire

They told us, sire, at the Pope's palace: "The hut of the holy hermit is on the slope of a hill, in the Roman Campagne, delineated against the sky, the profile of a ruined temple, and a clump of green oaks."

Robert

The Hermit is at his prayers. Stay here, my faithful squire. I will knock on his door.

Hermit

Who goes there? May the peace of heaven be with you.

Robert

I bring with me only the horrors of hell. Holy Hermit, will you receive me in confession?

Hermit

I beg you, my son, I don't confess anyone, especially great and proud lords like you.

Robert

Hermit, it is not a lord who comes to you, but a criminal. And, it was our Holy Father, the Pope in person, who, after having heard me, addressed me to you—so that you might inflict penitence on me.

Hermit

If such is the will of our Holy Father, kneel on the sill, my son, and confess. God hears!

Robert

Father, I confess only my sins. I will not invoke the infernal curse, which from the breast of my mother has hurled me into my atrocious life. As a child, I was a monster of cruelty, who tortured the other children

I played with, tore the entrails out of the dogs of the Duke, my father. As a young man, I tortured the peasants, polluted their marital beds, burned their cottages, sowed terror, misery, and shame. As a Knight, I commanded brigands, burned and pillaged monasteries, stole for pleasure the treasures of their chapels, sowed despair in the convents of the nuns, spilling so much innocent blood. I put out the eyes of the Barons who came to bring me the Duke's curse, and I sliced off the heads of seven saintly Hermits like you. Are you kicking me out, father? Is there nothing you can do? Are you raising your arms to heaven to curse me?

Hermit

No, my son. God alone can judge you. I am praying.

(The flute of a shepherd is heard and the baaing of his flock.)

Have you told me everything, my son? Here is your penitence. Because you've conducted yourself like a monster, you shall live like a beast. You will imitate the mute and the insane. You will only eat the food you've been able to steal from the jaws of dogs, even if you have to crawl in their holes. Whatever happens to you, even when varlets cover you with blows, even when children run after you and throw shit on you, you will accept it and pursue this abject life, so long as it pleases God our Lord. Go, penitent soul, and pray.

(The shepherd's flute is heard.)

BLACKOUT

SCENE VI

Before the palace of the Emperor. A great table is set.

Squire

Here I am, the poor Squire of Milord Robert, returning alone to the great city of Rome. Let's sit on this pillar in front of the palace. Before embarking on his terrible penitence, my poor young master, in a sweet voice, asked pardon and gave me my discharge. I will do nothing to interfere with the penance heaven has ordained. But, I swear, by the cloak of Saint Martin, that I will walk in his shadow, praying and begging my bread, if I must. Hey there, my good Water Carrier, what's this palace?

Water Carrier

Hey, what stranger? Don't you recognize the palace of the Emperor of Rome? With its staircases, its statues, its marble halls, and gold, open to all comers?

(The Emperor appears. One hears the blast of trumpets.)

Chamberlain

Milords, the Emperor.

Emperor

Now then, take your places, say your prayers and eat. Milords and Knights, I invite you. Behold the procession of our maîtres d'hôtel, who enter bearing plates of roasted pheasants, stuffed lamb, and smothered eels. (murmurs) But, tell me, Seneschal, what are those noises and shouting outside? Are my good people again demanding justice of me? At least, let them allow us time to appease our imperial appetite.

Seneschal

Lord Emperor, it is nothing. It's a man pursued by ragamuffin kids and the riff-raff, who scales your steps and penetrates into your palace.

Emperor

I see. They're always coming in here as if it were a public place.

(Enter Robert the Devil.)

God's wounds! What a handsome fellow. Look, under his torn clothes. That figure, that commanding bearing, those shoulders, that breast, that proud face. That, on my word, is the handsomest Knight, and the most beautiful man, I've ever seen. Hey, fellow! Are you hungry? Don't be afraid. It's the Emperor who speaks to you. And, at our table, there's always a share for the poor. God's share. Well, Seneschal? Why doesn't he approach when I order him? Why do all those vagrants continue to laugh on the steps of the palace?

(Murmurs.)

Seneschal

They say, Sire, that this man is mute and insane.

Emperor

That's a shame, Seneschal, but it's not a reason that a dad of this mold should be hungry in our palace. Hola, my squires and servants, let them give him something to eat and let him be served.

Seneschal

Sire, your servants have seated him at a table.

Emperor

I see. Eat, my friend. A beautiful body like yours needs to be supported. Holy Providence, what's he doing?

(Robert the Devil throws himself under the Emperor's table.)

Seneschal

Sire, he's thrown himself under the table on all fours, face to face with an enormous mastiff which is gnawing a bone. Oh, Lord Emperor, how marvelous. With his teeth, crawling on all fours, the mute is pulling the bone one way, while the dog, growling, is pulling it the other.

(Snarling from the dog.)

Emperor

Heavens, little Page. Hold my train. I want to see this. Give way, you others! Why, yes, on my oath, he's magnificent. I've never seen such a spectacle, even in my coliseum. What jaws! What a man. What do you have to say about it, Seneschal?

Seneschal

Lord Emperor, the mastiff is going to win. He's the strongest of your kennel. He can strangle a lion.

Emperor

Why, good God, the other one is tearing the bone from him, taking it away and chewing it. Go, go, my musicians. We are astonished, word of an Emperor, and this is worth more than a little tune.

(Murmurs and wailing.)

And, what's this here? I said my musicians. What are these discordant shouts?

Seneschal

Sire—

Emperor

Well, answer, Seneschal of the Palace, it's your function.

Seneschal

Sire, here's the chief of your armies.

(The Constable enters.)

Emperor

Well, Mr. Constable, answer.

Constable

Lord Emperor, they are the miscreants who are advancing anew, more numerous than the waves of the sea to attack Rome and Christianity.

Emperor

To arms! To arms, my Knights. To the ramparts. Let someone go request the Pope's blessing. And, let us all charge to the battle to save our city and the empire.

(Bells ring. Trumpets blare. Arms clash.)

SCENE VII

The garden on the mountain.

Squire

My master, my noble master, don't chase me away, and don't flee me! None can see us in this solitary garden on a hill dominating Rome, its ramparts, is churches, its palaces. Night has fallen. All day the battle has raged in the Campagne, all around the ramparts. Now the pagans form around campfires in the distance and the sounds of trumpets and Saracen drums can be heard. The weather's good here, Milord Robert, it's peaceful. Without interrupting your penance, you can rest your soul and pray in this deserted, somber garden. Down there, somewhere behind the cypresses, you can hear monks singing softly in the convent.

(Noise of distant singing and bells. In the distance, other songs and bells.)

Night and day, Rome prays for the victory of the Emperor and Christianity. And, I know you, Milord my master, if you have in your veins the devil's curse, you also have the heroic blood of the Duke of Normandy. Ho! Holy Mother. In this somber garden, lit only by the stars, what is that soft light coming and growing brighter? An Angel of Heaven is appearing before Robert the Devil! He carries in his arms a suit of armor, white like gold and stars, splendid, invulnerable and perfect in every point. Milord has fallen to his knees and joined his hands. Kyrie Eleison! The Angel is approaching again. He's going to speak.

Angel

Robert, heaven sees with what rigor you observe your penance. It knows what struggle it makes you lead against this body, bewitched by the curse that weighs upon it. Our Lord God does not release you from any of the chains of this penance. Remain mute. But, take this suit of armor, son of the Duke of Normandy. Run to the battle. Defend with your valor the right of Rome. Heaven orders you.

(The Angel vanishes.)

Squire

The Angel has disappeared. Robert the Devil prays, alone, silently before the shining armor. Here's the dawn. He puts on the white armor, descends the wall of the garden, finds attached to a tree, completely caparisoned in white, a battle charger with lance and sword hanging from the pommel of the saddle. The

Roman trumpets sound. The horns and cymbals of the Saracens resound. Magnificent, terrible, the White Knight rides down to the battling armies.

(Music.)

BLACKOUT

SCENE VIII

High above the ramparts of Rome, on the balcony of the Emperor's castle.

Emperor

My child, retire from this balcony. The arrows fill the air like flies. You might be wounded.

Princess

If my father, Lord Emperor, lets me see the battle, from this balcony which overlooks the ramparts, one can see everything as on a graven image. The armies line up and clash on the plain below your palace. Sire Emperor, Father! Father! Look! Our armies are collapsing. Our soldiers fall. I'm afraid.

Emperor

Go pray, my daughters. The place of a Princess is on her prie-dieu, and not on a balcony when the fate of an empire is in the hands of the Lord.

Princess

Sire Emperor, we must have help or we will perish. The Knights of Rome are succumbing under their number. The enemies are more numerous than the waves of the sea.

Emperor

Let them saddle my horse.

Princess

Father, Lord Father, look! Look! What is this miracle? A shining light is passing through the battle. A Knight wearing armor white like gold is charging into the ranks most heavy with Saracens. He's tracing, without respite, without cease, a new track. Look, Father! The heads are rolling, bodies collapsing. Rank after rank of enemies are falling.

(An Officer appears.)

Emperor

I see, my daughter. One has never before seen such a paladin under the sun. Come in, Officer. What news do you bring me?

Officer

Sire Emperor, victory hesitates, our troops are recovering. This White Knight, miraculously unexpected, is in the process of saving Rome and your army.

(Noises.)

Emperor

But, why are all these Knights running towards our ramparts? Hey, my loyal ones, are you running away from the battle?

Voices from Below the Walls

Lord Emperor, there is no more battle. Thanks to this unknown White Knight, all that is left is victory. The enemy is routed! Hear the cheers of our soldiers.

(Murmurs.)

Emperor

Let them bring the savior of Rome.

Princess

Oh! Father, yes, let them present this marvelous Knight.

Emperor

Well, my squires, my captains, you hesitate? You are waiting? You haven't gone yet?

Voices from Below the Walls

Sire, here's what we have still to tell you. The White Knight has vanished. He left as mysteriously as he came.

Emperor

Have him found! That's an order. And, on our right hand will sit this White Knight who has received the most illustrious Exploits of Roland, of Renard, and of the Paladin, Julius Caesar!

SCENE IX

By the fountain.

Princess

They've all gone. Let's stay here alone, my dear confidante—on this high balcony which overlooks the ramparts and the Campagne of Rome while our bells ring at random and the crowd sings and dances in the square.

(Distant bells.)

Confidante

Princess, my Princess, what can you be looking for now that the Campagne is deserted? Rather, listen, as throughout Rome the trumpets of the Heralds of your father resound everywhere.

Distant Voices

People and Lord. The Emperor of Rome lets it be known to all that he will give the hand of the Princess, his daughter, to the White Knight who saved Rome and Christianity. Let them speak!

(Fanfares.)

Princess

Oh, my dear confidante, look, as I do, down there. They are looking for the White Knight everywhere, and I really think we shall finally see him.

Confidante

Where, my Princess?

Princess

Down by that lovely fountain under the plane trees. He's left his shining armor and all his armor of victory.

Confidante

Yes, Princess. Why is he hiding them under the bushes?

Princess

I don't know. What's he doing now?

Confidante

He's bending over to drink some water from the fountain. Heavens! A Knight of the Emperor is passing by.

He's running at him full tilt. Doubtless he takes him for an enemy straggler.

Princess

Look, look again. I don't dare see. I've shut my eyes!

Confidante

Madame, the Emperor's Knight has struck the White Knight with his lance. He's left. Oh, the handsome Knight has fallen. The iron has entered deep into his thigh.

Princess

Is he alive? Answer! I will die if you don't speak.

Confidante

He's rising. He's tearing out the deeply stuck iron. He's dressing his wound. He's walking as he drinks. He's turning down the path. He's vanished.

Voices in the Distance

The Emperor of Rome makes it known that he will give the hand of the Princess, his daughter, to the White Knight.

BLACKOUT

SCENE X

The Throne Room.

Seneschal

Princess.

Princess

What do you wish, Seneschal?

Seneschal

Princess, before you enter the Throne Room where the Emperor invites all, allow me to make you a confidence.

Princess

That cannot wait, Seneschal?

Seneschal

You shall judge, Madame. I love you and count on asking your hand from the Emperor.

Princess

My hand, Milord, is no longer his nor mine, since my father's heralds have trumpeted throughout Rome that it belongs to the White Knight who saved Rome and Christianity.

Seneschal

And, if I were the White Knight?

Princess

That cannot be. He is wounded. But, the Emperor is signaling me from his throne. I must go sit by his side.

Emperor

Enter my loyalists and my vassals, my heroes! We will wait no longer for the White Knight before thanking heaven for our victory. Why are you whispering to me, my daughter? I can't hear a thing. Bend your head. Now, I can hear you.

Princess

Father, the White Knight, I saw him. He was wounded, wounded in the thigh. He took off his armor. He was drinking at the fountain below the palace. One of your officers passed by. He took him for an infidel! He struck him with his lance.

Emperor

Who lanced an unarmed Knight who was drinking from the fountain?

A Knight

Sire, Emperor, I am guilty and I am leaving to do penance in the Holy Land for having wounded, without realizing it, such a valorous Knight.

Seneschal

Don't leave, Chevalier, I pardon you.

Emperor

Who spoke? Why, it's our Seneschal? Well, he was drinking? He was wounded?

Seneschal

In the thigh, Sire.

Emperor

I think I understand. He is our hero, our White Knight. But, why all this heroic mystery?

Seneschal

For love of the Princess, Sire, that I wanted to deserve

and to win.

(The Squire of Robert the Devil appears.)

Squire

Lord Emperor, he's lying!

Emperor

Guards, bring me that Squire. Who are you?

Squire

I am the Squire of the White Knight, Sir. And, I know where the iron lance is that wounded my majesty! As for your Seneschal, from love for the Princess and perhaps, also, from love of the Empire he had the courage to pierce his thigh with an iron lance.

Emperor

Who, then is the truly wounded?

Princess

Father, I swear by God our Lord, the true wounded man, the real Knight, is mounting the steps of the palace, drinking. Here he is.

Voices

(laughter, murmurs.) Ha, ha, it's the mute. The Dog-Man. Where's he from? He's drinking.

(Robert the Devil enters, humble and mute.)

Emperor

Come, Princess, come, come, my child. According to you, this is the magnificent, but mad and mute champion, who will be our hero? You're crazy in your turn. But, who is scaling our steps blessing the people?

(The Hermit appears.)

An Officer

Sire, it's the Holy Hermit from the mountain.

Emperor

Before you, Holy Hermit, the Emperor himself can rise. Besides, this is the first time you've left your retreat to enter our palace.

Hermit

Why, it's by order of God our Lord, Lord Emperor. Before you, Emperor of Rome, and you, noble Princess, and you, Lords and Knights, stands, overwhelmed by silence, this mute Lord who falls at my feet. Rise,

Robert, Duke of Normandy! Your penitence and your sincerity have appeased heaven. You are freed from the diabolic sorcery which weighed on you. Your penance is completed. God our Sovereign has agreed to it. In the future, be just, you who were Robert the Devil. Be good. And protect, with your strong arm, Christianity.

Emperor

Come, Robert, Duke of Normandy. Your penitence has led you to our victory. Give me your hand. My daughter, here is the savior of Rome and of our throne! I have only one word.

Princess

Father, my Lord, I heard the announcement made by your Heralds. I will be honored to keep your word.

People (in the distance)

Long live our Savior, the Duke of Normandy.

Robert

Madame, I will try to deserve the grace heaven has shed on me and that granted to me your beauty.

(Music.)

CURTAIN

ABOUT THE AUTHOR

Frank J. Morlock has written and translated many plays since retiring from the legal profession in 1992. His translations have also appeared on Project Gutenberg, the Alexandre Dumas Père web page, Literature in the Age of Napoléon, Infinite Artistries.com, and Munsey's (formerly Blackmask). In 2006 he received an award from the North American Jules Verne Society for his translations of Verne's plays. He lives and works in México.

www.ingramcontent.com/pod-product-compliance
Lightning Source LLC
LaVergne TN
LVHW041615070426
835507LV00008B/259